Erotographomania:
Love Letters to M.

C. R. Andrews

Copyright © 2016 Christopher Andrews
Radiant Sky Publishing Group
All rights reserved.

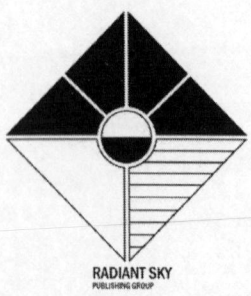

ISBN- 978-0692609163
ISBN-0692609164

DEDICATION

For you.

Erotographomania: Love Letters to M.

Erotographomania.

n. A compulsive desire to write love letters or love poems, commonly in connection with sexual arousal.

C.R. Andrews

Erotographomania: Love Letters to M.

i need to show you
i need you to see
the fawning
the tales of lust
the words of hope
and wanting
the rapture of your beauty
you need to learn
that it is all true.

it is time you knew.

Erotographomania: Love Letters to M.

INTRODUCTION

C.R. Andrews

Erotographomania: Love Letters to M.

Let me start by saying that all of these letters are real. What you see on the cover are the actual letters. The ones in her possession. Out of all of my published and unpublished work, this is the first time when the original papers are not in my hands. They were never meant to be kept. They are for her. Initially, there was never even an intent to publish these. But my medium for expressing my love for M had shifted. It had evolved. And I wanted the world to know it. I felt that I had expressed my love in every possible way. I used every metaphor and simile that I could muster. And with every word I delivered, my chest would swell and my egomania would be sated as I watched and listened to her soak up every syllable, every word, and every letter. But she needed more. I needed to give more. I needed her to want more. The only thing that fed me night after night was to write for her. For my M. Eternally searching for the right words. Sometimes I would write for her and be out of breath by the time I put the pencil down. My head would swim with vanity that I finally wrote something worthy of her beauty, and as I wrote I would tremble from the fear of how she would receive it. It was exhausting. I couldn't stop. Not only did I torture myself each time by thinking I didn't express myself strongly enough, that what I wrote was not worthy of her, but each time I feared if I stopped or said it the wrong way that I would lose her.

Erotographomania was a term I was not even familiar with until the past year or so. I learned it from listening to an old series of lectures given by the great Nick Cave called *The Secret Life of the Love Song*. These lectures had become my "go to" background noise for writing, editing, composing, brooding, reflecting, pouting, drinking, or anything else. I remember when I first heard the description of erotographomania along with the description of the afflicted that was referenced and feeling so sorry for the poor soul and at the same time I was so incredibly jealous. Then I realized that this is exactly what had happened to me. I was not only obsessed with M but the compulsion to keep writing only grew stronger.

I had already been writing poetry for M for quite some time. Almost all of the love poems in *Learning to Lasso the Moon* were for her, and during the time featured here I was still writing poetry for her. But now by adding the lost tradition of handwritten love letters into the mix, I had yet another outlet to feed my addiction to her. At this point, my outlets had now become limitless.

Erotographomania: Love Letters to M.

C.R. Andrews

Erotographomania: Love Letters to M.

i don't care how
pointless this is
i don't care if
i can't have you
i will never bury this
i will live absent
of kiss
i will live absent
of touch
there is simply
no
other choice.

7/30/15

Dearest M.

These letters are for you to read now while this love is still fresh. While we can still taste the desire in the air. While new songs become our songs. And we mark new places and create new stories forever owned by only you and I. These letters are to capture this time before we are forced to let go of each other. To preserve these perfect memories for when you are old. When you pull these from an old shoebox under the bed, you can remember again of the summer that we loved with fierce anger and foolish adoration.

          Love, C.

Erotographomania: Love Letters to M.

30 Sep 2015

Dearest M.

These letters are for you to read now while this love is still fresh. While we can still taste the desire in the air. While new songs become our songs and we mark new places and create new stories forever owned by only you and I. These letters are to capture this time before we are forced to let go of each other. To preserve these perfect memories for when you are old. When you pull these from an old shoebox under your bed, you can remember again of the summer that we loved with fierce anger and foolish adoration.

Love, C.

9/30/15

Dearest M,

I remember how we made our way through the city that night. Every man looked at us incredulously, wondering how you were mine. You didn't even realize how I was flaunting you about. They turned their heads at us and I looked back with a grin that was both smug and predatory. The bridge, the fountain, the stairs, the dark path by the pier where murders happen. You were always safe that night. And that night you were always mine.

     Love, C.

Erotographomania: Love Letters to M.

30 Sep 2015

Dearest M.

I remember how we made our way through the city that night. Every man looked at us incredulously, wondering how you were mine. You didn't even realize how I was flaunting you about. They turned their heads at us and I looked back with a grin that was both smug and predatory. The bridge, the fountain, the stairs, the dark path by the pier where murders happen. You were always safe that night. And that night you were always mine.

Love, C.

10/1/15

Dearest M.

I remember you crossed your arms and looked away. Your voice got softer and trailed off. Your thoughts drifting to another place you weren't ready to share with me yet. I wasn't sure how to comfort you. We were still stuck in the newness of things being undefined. I didn't know what was appropriate which made everything inappropriate. But that is when it started. That was the moment that I knew from that moment on that every time I was in your presence would be a struggle to not be touching you in some way.

Love, C.

Erotographomania: Love Letters to M.

1 Oct 2015

Dearest M.

I remember you crossed your arms and looked away. Your voice got softer and trailed off. Your thoughts drifting to another place you weren't ready to share with me yet. I wasn't sure how to comfort you. We were still stuck in the newness of things being undefined. I didn't know what was inappropriate which made everything inappropriate. But that is when it started. That was the moment I knew that from that moment on, every time I was in your presence would be a struggle to not be touching you in some way.

Love, C.

10/1/15

Dearest M.

There were so many times for us to share that first touch, that first kiss. I could have reached over and put my arm around your waist. Hooked my fingers into your belt loops and pulled you against me. There was that moment when I pushed your hair off of your shoulder. So many times that our lips should have met that night. Those moments of silence that were meant for that moment. Am I afraid of rejection or are you just afraid that you wouldn't want to stop me?

Love, C.

Erotographomania: Love Letters to M.

01 Oct 2015

Dearest M.

There were so many times for us to share that first touch. That first kiss. I could have reached over and put my arm around your waist. Hooked my fingers into your belt loops and pulled you against me. There was that moment when I pushed your hair off of your shoulder. So many times our lips should have met that night. Those moments of silence that were meant for that moment. Am I afraid of rejection or are you just afraid that you wouldn't want to stop me?

Love, C.

10/2/15

Dearest M.,

I thought of the most ridiculous things today. Innocuous things that the average person takes for granted. People-watching at the park and in restaurants. Arguing over flavors of ice cream at the grocery store. Me mocking your laugh and you mocking my rants on pointless subjects. Lazy Sundays of crossword puzzles and watching bad Kurt Russell movies in bed. The moments when my actions are such a nonsensical disaster and your only response is to laugh, shake your head, and say, "I adore you"

Love, C.

Erotographomania: Love Letters to M.

2 Oct 2015

Dearest M.

I thought of the most ridiculous things today. Innocuous things that the average person takes for granted. People-watching at the park and in restaurants. Arguing over flavors of ice cream at the grocery store. Me mocking your laugh and you mocking my rants on pointless subjects. Lazy Sundays of crossword puzzles and watching bad Kurt Russell movies in bed. The moments when my actions are such a nonsensical disaster and your only response is to laugh, shake your head, and say "I adore you."

Love, C.

10/8/15

Dearest M,
We have to endure so many of these days in between the nights we can spend together. As much as it pains me, these are the times that remind me what love is. The days and nights of your absence only draw me closer to you. Because we both know that soon enough you will be here. What I fear is not the day when we take our time together for granted but when we take the time apart for granted. I want us to never feel comfort. I want us to never learn patience. I want every moment apart to be just as maddening as waiting for that first kiss.
          Love, C.

Erotographomania: Love Letters to M.

3 Oct 2015

Dearest M.

We have to endure so many of these days in between the nights we can spend together. As much as it pains me, these are the times that remind me what love is. The days and nights of your absence only draw me closer to you. Because we both know that soon enough you will be here. What I fear is not the day when we take our time together for granted but when we take the time apart for granted. I want us to never feel comfort. I want us to never learn patience. I want every moment apart to be just as maddening as waiting for that first kiss.

Love, C.

10/4/15

Dearest M,

I've always loved this house. I keep it meticulously clean and organized most of the time. It's decorated to be warm and cozy, but it has started to fall into disarray. It has always assumed the imminent presence of another. And now it defiantly demands it. Not any presence, but your presence. Everything within these walls I have made for two. For you. What good is this loveseat? What good is this dining room table with a single plate? What good is this fireplace warming only my body? What good is this bed without you wrapped in the sheets? What good is the morning sun through the window when it is not on your beautiful face?

Love, C.

Erotographomania: Love Letters to M.

4 Oct 2015

Dearest M.

I've always loved this house. I keep it meticulously clean and organized most of the time. It's decorated to be warm and cozy. But it has started to fall into disarray. It has always assumed the imminent presence of another. And now, it defiantly demands it. Not any presence, but your presence. Everything within these walls I have made for two. For you. What good is this loveseat? What good is a dining room table with a single plate? What good is this fireplace warming only my body? What good is this bed without you wrapped in the sheets? What good is the morning sun through the window when it is not shining on your beautiful face?

Love, C.

10/4/15

Dearest M.,

I know now why I stay up so late at night. I dont want to open that door to the bedroom and see you not there. I wont get to hear that little moan when you sleepily tell me to turn the fucking light off. I wont feel your perfect naked body back up and settle in against me. We both know I dont dream and when I close my eyes for the night you are gone. I only toss and turn and awaken gasping for air so I can once again return to this longing.

Love, C.

Erotographomania: Love Letters to M.

4 Oct 2015

Dearest M.

I know now why I stay up so late at night. I don't want to open that door to the bedroom and see you not there. I won't get to hear that little moan when you sleepily tell me to turn the fucking light off. I won't feel your perfect naked body back up and settle in against me. We both know I don't dream and when I close my eyes for the night you are gone. I only toss and turn and awake gasping for air so I can once again return to this longing.

Love, C.

10/5/15

Dearest M,
It's one of those nights again. It's stronger than usual. It is one of those nights where your picture and your memory is not enough, where the memory of your scent is not enough, where the sound of your voice dancing through the wires is not enough, where knowing that the dwindling days between the time when I can see you again strengthens not longing but yet deepens madness. Madness from the hunger and from the fear that you might say goodbye. I am tricking death with each day that I get closer to your arms again.

                Love, C.

5 Oct 2015

Dearest M.

It's one of those nights again. It's stronger than usual. It is one of those nights where your picture and your memory is not enough. Where the memory of your scent is not enough. Where the sound of your voice dancing through the wires is not enough. Where knowing that the dwindling days between the time when I can see you again strengthens not longing but deepens madness. Madness from the hunger and from the fear that you might say goodbye. I am tricking death with each day that I get closer to your arms again.

Love, C.

10/9/15

Dearest M.,

This was one of those rare nights where I smiled. It was a night for celebrating. I know you couldn't be here but I still felt you here. You listened to me going on and on about baseball even though you couldn't care less about the subject. It brought you such joy just to witness me being excited about something. You just let me go on and on. You were never just patronizing me. It actually mattered. I forgot what it was like to not feel as if everything out of my mouth was just an annoyance. You had never said the words, but that is when I knew you loved me.

               Love, C.

Erotographomania: Love Letters to M.

9 Oct 2015

Dearest M.

This was one of those rare nights where I smiled. It was a night for celebrating. I know you couldn't be here but I still felt you here. You listened to me going on and on about baseball even though you couldn't care less about the subject. It brought you such joy just to witness me being excited about something. You just let me go on and on. You were never just patronizing me. It actually mattered. I forgot what it was like to not feel as if everything out of my mouth was just an annoyance. You had never said the words, but that is when I knew you loved me

Love, C.

10/9/15

Dearest M.

You know I didn't even realize I was laughing until you told me we rewrote the worst poems we could find and managed to make them even worse. Oh how we laughed. We are such assholes. And there is nobody I would rather be this hateful and inappropriate with. I had forgotten my laugh. But you brought it back. Not my normal laugh but the real one. The belly laugh with tears. The one that hurts. And yet you still wonder if and why I love you

Love, C.

Erotographomania: Love Letters to M.

09 Oct 2015

Dearest M.

You know I didn't even realize I was laughing until you told me. We rewrote the worst poems we could find and managed to make them even worse. Oh how we laughed. We are such assholes. And there is nobody I would rather be this hateful and inappropriate with. I had forgotten my laugh. But you brought it back. Not my normal laugh but the real one. The belly laugh with tears. The one that hurts. And you still wonder why I love you.

Love, C.

10/11/15

Dearest M.

This is the letter I knew I would eventually have to write, but the one I hoped I never would. Yet here we are. Love isn't always enough. This time it ended with a whimper as well as a bang. This is the last letter I will write you. I will walk away with no regrets. I'll never question why I gave all to one I can't have. If it was a rational thought then it simply wouldn't be love. Though we part, I know that we do it with you finally knowing you were loved. And it had to come to this before you could finally say "I love you Christopher." And those parting words made all of this worth everything

Love, C.

Erotographomania: Love Letters to M.

11 Oct 2015

Dearest M.

This is the letter I knew I would eventually have to write, but the one I hoped I never would. Yet here we are. Love isn't always enough. This time it ended with a whimper as well as a bang. This is the last letter I will write you. I will walk away with no regrets. I'll never question why I gave all to one I can't have. If it was a rational thought then it simply wouldn't be love. Though we part, I know that we do it with you finally knowing that you were loved. And it had to come to this before you could finally say "I love you Christopher." And those parting words made all of this worth everything.

Love, C.

Erotographomania: Love Letters to M.

INTERLUDE

C.R. Andrews

Erotographomania: Love Letters to M.

i have been trying to
spread my thoughts
so thinly
everywhere but with
one woman
yet now
they are all
only hungry
for you.

C.R. Andrews

At this point, writing for a woman was nothing new. I had been doing it since I was a teenager. Of course, thankfully, I got a little better at it over the years. Most of my work has been for a woman. Hit one of my poems with a dart and I'll tell you her name. I'll tell you the when and the where. This is what I do. This is what I have always done.

Some got more than one poem. Most of them got a couple. Three was rare. More than that and chances are it was a few love poems and the rest were bitter and scathing hate-filled takedown pieces after the subject ultimately broke my heart. But as I learned, I could never write such hate if I never knew their love. No, I am not going to launch into a cliché about hate being based in love. I have hated plenty of people where love never existed. You can hate without love. But when you hate one that you once loved it is a hate that is tenfold what it would be without love. There is no deeper pain and no deeper hate that one can feel than that for the one you once worshipped. Like disowning the mother and father that gave you life. Like the betrayal of the priest that brought you into the light of Christ. That hate, that hell, that torment, that betrayal, is what happens in the absence of love. With love being ripped from your life. But you will always move past the hate. You don't have to forgive. You don't have to forget. You don't have to look back and savor the good times. But you will always learn something. You can continue to love and you can continue to despise that person. But you will love again. You have to.

I find it fascinating that there is so much weight put on how many times one has been in love. As if only saying the words "I love you" once means more than when it came from a person who has said it a dozen times. Yes, there is romance in the tragedy of Romeo and Juliet. We swoon over the lovers who exclaim "I will never love again." Don't get me wrong. I admire that kind of love. I've felt it. And I have felt it more than once. I have wished death upon myself again and again because of love. But I made it out. This is one of the many problems we have in our view of romantic love. That in order for it to be true it has to be an undying love that ruins you for all others. That each time you say "I love you" it somehow means less than when you said it before. This is, quite simply, utter nonsense. I have no shame in saying that off the top of my head, I can name 14 women I was in love with. Yes that sounds like a lot.

Keep in mind that this was also over a period of 30 years. But even so, 14 women sounds like a lot doesn't it? You are already shaking your head. My view of love is already diminished to you. I was in a conversation with a group of friends recently and everyone had the same story. "I've only said it once," "I've only said it twice." And even the person who admitted to saying it to two people came with a disclaimer. Personally, I pity those people. We almost never win at love the first time. And even when that love doesn't end in disaster we can still be wrong. Yet the end isn't always wrong and it isn't always a mistake. I loved many women before my ex-wife. She and I ended up together for 17 years until it ended. But it was not a failure. It was not a failed marriage. We made it longer than most. Why does the end have to mean failure? I loved before and I have loved since. This has no bearing on my love for my former wife, the subsequent loves, or Jami Schatz from 6th grade homeroom.

So, what does this have to do with M? I'll tell you. I have lost at love again and again. I have sworn before that someone was my one and only. I meant it every time. And I knew each time there was the potential for disaster; for falling apart again. But I will jump in every time. This world is full of beautiful and wonderful people. I pity you if you feel you missed out on "the one." I'm here to tell you that there is no such thing. Perhaps I shouldn't put it that way. We all have "the one." But you have to get over the stigma of missing out on the first try. Or the second, or third, or tenth. Look back and think of the one that got away because you felt it was too soon. Because you weren't ready to give your heart again. Now I want you to recognize when you do it again and throw yourself into that fucking pit. Jump into the fire soaked in gasoline. If you feel something, if you feel anything, then embrace it. Feet first, head first, face first, leap right into that love. Dive right into the stupidity. Abandon everything over and over again in the hope that this was the right time. Fuck rationality. Fuck convention. Fuck popular opinion. Fuck everything. Make yourself look like a G-d damned fool. And even if it turns out to be the wrong choice, fucking do it again. When it comes to love there is no crime. You are allowed everything. This is the one time when everything is acceptable and forgivable.

Show every lover your brightest and darkest side. Do it again and again. You will know it is right when someone allows you to do it. M did this for me. She burned down the history of any woman that ever touched me. She destroyed the words of fleeting love that came from the ones before her. How sad it would be if I diminished her love because I wasted time on what happened before her. How stupid I would be to restrain my love for a woman like this because of someone before her who took it for granted. Ruin yourself. Go for everything all the time.

Be willing for love to die. Be willing to let it die to be reborn again. Be willing to let love in every single fucking time.

Erotographomania: Love Letters to M.

Erotographomania: Love Letters to M.

we are all getting older
and you and i are lucky that
the years have been kind
but we don't have many left
more than half our lives
have passed now
we can't afford to waste
more years
more months
more days
let's make this time for us
every single moment that
we can steal from the ones
who are too afraid
to dream.

10/13/15

Dearest M.,

I tried to say goodbye to you. I tried to stay away from you. But damn you and your voice. Your face. The parts of you that make me so weak. But there is nothing rational with you. There is no restraint. There is nothing in me that can take a step away. I fear nothing in this world could make me distance myself from you. There is no rationale. There is no logic. I am forever shackled to you until the day you decide it is time to send me to the slaughter.

Love, C.

Erotographomania: Love Letters to M.

13 Oct 2015

Dearest M.

I tried to say goodbye to you. I tried to stay away from you. But damn you and your voice. Your face. The parts of you that make me so weak. But there is nothing rational with you. There is no restraint. There is nothing in me that can take a step away. I fear nothing in this world could make me distance myself from you. There is no rationale. There is no logic. I am forever shackled to you until the day you decide it is time to send me to the slaughter.

Love, C.

Dearest M, 10/15/15

So much has changed since I last saw you. I never thought we would grow to this level. But somewhere between now and an awkward beginning, we fell in love. I don't know when we fell for each other, who fell first. At this point is doesn't matter. Here we are. I said it. You said it. I won you. I won the prize I thought was unwinnable. I convinced the one who felt unloveable that she was loved. I possess a treasure that not only is no man worthy of, but one that was impossible to find. You are mine. You are all mine. You are only mine.

Love, C.

Erotographomania: Love Letters to M.

15 Oct 2015

Dearest M.

So much has changed since I last saw you. I never thought we would grow to this level. But somewhere between now and an awkward beginning, we fell in love. I don't know when we fell for each other, who fell first. At this point it doesn't matter. Here we are. I said it. You said it. I won you. I won the prize I thought was unwinnable. I convinced the one who felt unlovable that she was loved. I possess a treasure that not only is no man worthy of, but one that was impossible to find. You are mine. You are all mine. You are only mine.

Love, C.

10/05/15

Dearest M.,

I wish for once you could be selfish. Somewhere along the line that word has become a bad thing. It simply means doing something that pleases you or something that puts your own interests first. You can't live a life of sacrifice. At some point, it's time to allow yourself to live. And aren't our so-called selfless acts often selfish by nature? We sacrifice our own needs and put those of others first because it pleases us to do so. We feel like we are better people for doing it. Or we do it to avoid a crippling feeling of guilt. Our unwillingness to bring that burden on ourselves is even stronger that choosing happiness. Isn't that a more selfish act?

Love, C.

15 Oct 2015

Dearest M.

I wish for once you could be selfish. Somewhere along the line that word has become a bad thing. It simply means doing something that pleases you or something that puts your own interests first. You can't live a life of sacrifice. At some point, it's time to allow yourself to live. And aren't our so-called selfless acts often selfish by nature? We sacrifice our own needs and put those of others first because it pleases us to do so. We feel like we are better people for doing it. Or we do it to avoid a crippling feeling of guilt. Our unwillingness to bring this burden on ourselves is even stronger than choosing happiness. Isn't that a mere selfish act?

Love, C.

10/23/15

Dearest M,
Each night you aren't in my bed gets exponentially unbearable. But for now I know we have to live for those few days and nights we can have. Rationing our smiles, our kisses, our laughter, and our wanting embrace. I'm waiting for the day when none of this matters. This will all be a distant memory. When Friday nights are eating pizza and watching 80's movies in a bed full of cats. When mornings are no longer me reaching out to sunlight and empty spaces but reaching out to pull my lover closer against me. Reunited at every crack of dawn.
 Love, C.

Erotographomania: Love Letters to M.

23 Oct 2015

Dearest M.

Each night you aren't in my bed gets exponentially unbearable. But for now I know we have to live for those few days and nights we can have. Rationing our smiles, our kisses, our laughter, and our wanting embrace. I'm waiting for the day when none of this matters. This will all be a distant memory. When Friday nights are eating pizza and watching 80's movies in a bed full of cats. When mornings are no longer reaching out to sunlight and empty space but reaching out to pull my lover closer against me. Reunited at every crack of dawn.

Love, C.

C.R. Andrews

10/24/2015

Dearest M.

How much longer do we need to wait? How long do we deny everything that we already know to be true? You belong here. I know it. You know it. This is the fairytale. This is the beauty that comes from tragedy. We are the least likely to make it. The least likely to succeed. And we are the ones to show everyone that convention and logic is wrong. We are the ones that defy all odds and all rational thought. We are the unloved. The unlovable. We are the only ones who could love each other. Let us not live a life wondering or regretting. Let us be the fools, the reckless, the insane, and the lovers that every god would despise.

Love, C.

Erotographomania: Love Letters to M.

24 Oct 2015

Dearest M.

How much longer do we need to wait? How long do we deny everything that we already know to be true? You belong here. I know it. You know it. This is the fairytale. This is the beauty that comes from tragedy. We are the least likely to succeed. And we are the ones to show everyone that convention and logic is wrong. We are the ones to defy all odds and all rational thought. We are the unloved. The unlovable. We are the only ones who could love each other. Let us not live a life wondering or regretting. Let us be the fools, the reckless, the insane, and the lovers that every god would despise.

Love, C.

10/25/2015

Dearest M.

It still amazes me how your face, your smile, and your body always seems like such a new thing. Every curve and every movement of your mouth is like the moment I first broke through these barriers. My hand on your body is always new, always different. Sliding down your neck, tracing your collarbone, gliding down your breasts, your ribcage, the curve of your small but round hips, is always new and thrilling. I'm always finding a new slope, a new inch, a new detail of your body that I want to claim. I am still in awe of what belongs to me and the years I now get to covet it.

Love, C.

Erotographomania: Love Letters to M.

25 Oct 2015

Dearest M.

It still amazes me how your face, your smile, and your body always seems like such a new thing. Every laugh and every movement of your mouth is like the moment I first broke though those barriers. My hand on your body is always new, always different. Sliding down your neck, tracing your collarbone, gliding down your breasts, your ribcage, the curve of your small but round hips, is always new and thrilling. I'm always finding a new slope, a new inch, a new detail of your body that I want to claim. I am still in awe of what belongs to me and the years I now get to covet it.

Love, C.

11/2/15

Dearest M.

Until now, I never wanted to touch anyone again. I lost all desire, I lost all my nerve, I lost any confidence that was left. And I accepted that life. But you changed all that. The pools of your eyes are the Lazarus Pit. Your skin is a virgin star. Your mouth is the cup of Christ. You remind a man how to be a man. You remind me what we are here for. You are the end of a crucible and proof that nobody can ever destroy the capacity for love.

          Love, C.

Erotographomania: Love Letters to M.

2 Nov 2015

Dearest M.

Until now I never wanted to touch anyone again. I lost all desire. I lost all my nerve. I lost any confidence that was left. And I accepted that life. But you changed all that. The pools of your eyes are the Lazarus pit. Your skin is a virgin star. Your mouth is the cup of Christ. You remind a man how to be a man. You remind me what we are here for. You are the end of a crucible and proof that nobody can ever destroy the capacity for love.

Love, C.

11/14/15

Dearest M.

Do you remember the first night that I touched you? It was innocent enough. I just reached around your neck and brushed the hair from your shoulder, and away from your face. That was all it took for me to be lost in you. I could still feel the softness of your hair. I could still smell your shampoo. I still feel the sensation that went through my body when my fingertips ever so slightly touched your cheek. I never thought it would be more than that. But now here you are with the dawn gracing your face next to me, the scent of you taking over the pillow case, and your panties lost on under the covers at the foot of the bed

Love, C.

Erotographomania: Love Letters to M.

14 Nov 2015

Dearest M.

Do you remember the first night that I touched you? It was innocent enough. I just reached around your neck and brushed the hair from your face. That was all it took for me to be lost in you. I could still feel the softness of your hair. I could still smell your shampoo. I still feel the sensation that went through my body when my fingertips ever so slightly touched your cheek. I never thought it would be more than that. But now here you are with the dawn gracing your face next to me, the scent of you taking over the pillowcase, and your panties lost under the covers at the foot of the bed.

Love, C.

11/22/15

Dearest M.

I'm sorry. I never meant it to be this way. It wasn't supposed to be an obsession. But I don't care anymore. I don't care who knows it. I don't care about our stupidity or our futility. Nothing will keep me from you. Nothing will keep me from saying your name to everyone I meet. Nothing will stop me from showing everyone that you are mine. My girl. My love. I want people to see us and hate us. I want them to be disgusted by how we fawn over each other. I want people to see what we have and make their lives feel empty.

Love, C.

Erotographomania: Love Letters to M.

22 Nov 2015

Dearest M.

I'm sorry. I never meant it to be this way. It wasn't supposed to be an obsession. But I don't care anymore. I don't care who knows it. I don't care about our stupidity or our futility. Nothing will keep me from you. Nothing will keep me from saying your name to everyone I meet. Nothing will stop me from showing everyone that you are mine. My girl. My love. I want people to see us and hate us. I want them to be disgusted by how we fawn over each other. I want people to see what we have and make their lives feel empty.

Love, C.

12/2/15

Dearest M.

You need to be here. Not tonight. Not tomorrow. Not this weekend. Every night. Every day. I need to see that face every morning. I need to kiss your head and put the comforter up over your shoulder before I leave for work. I need to walk in the door at the end of the day and see you on the sofa curled up with one of the cats and wearing nothing but one of my T-shirts. I need you to hit the pause button on the remote and run to the door and kiss me as if 10 hours were 10 days apart. I need your joy from the sight of me to never grow old.

Love, C.

Erotographomania: Love Letters to M.

2 Dec 2015

Dearest M.

You need to be here. Not tonight. Not tomorrow. Not this weekend. Every night. Every day. I need to see that face every morning. I need to kiss your head and put the comforter up over your shoulder before I leave for work. I need to walk in the door at the end of the day and see you on the sofa curled up with one of the cats and wearing nothing but one of my t-shirts. I need you to hit the pause button on the remote and run to the door and kiss me as if 10 hours were 10 days apart. I need your joy from the sight of me to never grow old.

Love, C.

12/2/15

Dearest M,

Wherever we go, nobody will doubt that you are mine. The slightest glimpse of us together will scream "This is my girl."

Men will scoff to hide their envy, women will sneer with jealousy knowing they will never be as beautiful as you. They will never be looked at the way I look at you. They will never be worshipped the way I worship you. My adoration of you is pure and shameless arrogance. I will flaunt your beauty and our love in the most obnoxious ways. You are my girl. Everyone will know. I love you. I adore you. I covet you. You are mine

Love, C.

Erotographomania: Love Letters to M.

2 Dec 2015

Dearest M.

Wherever we go, nobody will doubt that you are mine. The slightest glimpse of us together will scream "this is my girl." Men will scoff to hide their envy. Women will sneer with jealousy knowing they will never be as beautiful as you. They will never be looked at the way I look at you. They will never be worshipped the way I worship you. My adoration of you is pure and shameless arrogance. I will flaunt your beauty and our love in the most obnoxious ways. You are my girl. Everyone will know. I love you. I adore you. I covet you. You are mine.

Love, C.

12/6/15

Dearest M,

Sometimes I wonder if you becoming a part of my life in middle age is proof that it is never too late. That we just had to be patient all these years and everything in our lives was to lead us to this time. Even 20 years ago something was starting a long path for us to walk upon to finally end up in each other's arms. Or is it an example of how cruel and unfair life can be? How we were robbed of decades of memories? How pictures on the wall and momentos in shoe boxes should be overwhelmed with our life together? I want to fill those frames, I want to fill those boxes.
        Love, C.

Erotographomania: Love Letters to M.

6 Dec 2015

Dearest M.

Sometimes I wonder if you becoming a part of my life in middle age is proof that it is never too late. That we just had to be patient all these years and everything in our lives was to lead us to this time. Even 20 years ago something was starting a long path for us to walk upon to finally end up in each other's arms. Or is it an example of how cruel and unfair life can be? How we were robbed of decades of memories? How pictures on the wall and mementos in shoe boxes should be overwhelmed with our life together? I want to fill those frames. I want to fill those boxes.

Love, C.

12/11/15

Dearest M,

I've only been in this house for two years, my fresh start, but there are already memories. There are already ghosts and echoes, but some things are still untouched. There is still room for something to be created. There is room for your new scent to overtake these spaces. There are walls that need a new voice. They are ready to drip with your words and our memories. The carpet is waiting for lost strands of your hair. The light switch is waiting for your fingertips. The glow of the television is waiting for your sleepy eyes to flutter and close. Cats are waiting to purr on your lap. This is your home now. This is our home. And it is ready to swell with our future.

Love, C.

Erotographomania: Love Letters to M.

11 Dec 2015

Dearest M.

I've only been in this house for two years. My fresh start. But there are already memories. There are already ghosts and echoes. But some things are still untouched. There is still room for something to be created. There is room for your new scent to overtake these spaces. There are walls that need a new voice. They are ready to drip with your words and our memories. The carpet is waiting for the lost strands of your hair. The light switch is waiting for your fingertips. The glow of the television is waiting for your sleepy eyes to flutter and close. Cats are waiting to purr on your lap. This is your home now. This is our home. And it is ready to swell with our future.

Love, C.

CONCLUSION

Erotographomania: Love Letters to M.

Now my friends it is the time for the big reveal. After all this you might be wondering what became of C and M. Well, yes we were deeply in love but no, we did not live happily ever after. You see, M was never mine. She belongs to someone else. She always did. What you have just read is both very real and very much a fantasy. Do I regret it? No, I don't. She brought me back to life. That is the whole point here. We must always be willing to pursue the most foolish love. The pointless love. We must remember how to be alive. We have to learn that you can only be free to love when you are not only prepared for but willing to risk what might be imminent suffering. Which, once again goes back to the lectures I listened to over and over that only made sense in theory until now. You get the girl or you don't get the girl. Either way there is pain. There is suffering. And I am suffering for M. A suffering and a longing that can't be defined in conventional words of the English language. What the Portuguese describe as saudade[1], and Lorca's theory of duende[2]. I gave everything shamelessly.

Here is the thing with M, I knew from the beginning that it was impossible. I knew this fantasy world we created would not last. I knew it would end and that it would end with two very lonely and broken people. I found her at the darkest time in my life. Yet I chose to let myself be enveloped in the aura of a woman I would never have. I knew at some point she and I would both have to accept this and say goodbye to what we had. But this was something too powerful to ignore. At 42 years old when I thought I had felt everything a man could possibly feel, I met M. I thought so many times before that I had given everything and all those times are now a fraction of what I gave to M and what I revealed of myself to her. With all of the women I've loved, not one has brought this much out of me. It started with one poem of simple admiration. A crush. Then it grew to 10. Then 20. Then 50. It grew until this woman had pulled thousands of words from me; tens of

---

[1] Saudade describes a deep emotional state of nostalgic or profound melancholic longing for something that is absent or someone that one loves..

[2] In *Theory and Play of the Duende* Lorca spoke of duende as being the inspiration and the darkness that lives in certain forms of artistic expression. It is often said to be the most difficult word to translate from Spanish to English. Simply and loosely translated it is a heightened state of passion, emotion, and inspiration. Lorca describes three spiritual entities that inspire all creativity: muses, angels, and duende. Duende being something everyone feels but nobody can define or explain.

thousands. My love for her is immeasurable. The combination of words infinite. They would never be enough. I will go to my grave never being able to feel I did her justice. But this was not just for me. It was not about how I loved her and my ability to express it in a previously unparalleled way. She deserved it. She commanded it. I could not sit by and watch until M knew exactly what a wonder she was to behold. She deserved, and still deserves, to be worshipped. To be adored. To be shown that she truly is one of the beautiful ones. And now that it is over, that we both have accepted what will never be, all I can hope for is that sometimes I will creep into her thoughts. That sometimes I will slip into her deepest dreams. That I will find my way into her conscious daydreams. That she will be able to look back and smile. That she will feel warm. That she will feel and remember our uncontainable, delirious, hopeless, and blissfully doomed love. The words we still never found. The plateau we never reached. The saudade, the duende, and all things left undiscovered and undefined but always felt to the point of madness.

Erotographomania: Love Letters to M.

i don't want to sleep
i don't want to be
in that room or
in that bed with
nothing but a picture on
the nightstand and
and old tank top with
the fading smell of
your perfume
to remind me that
another man has
the real thing
so i sleep
and i dream
dreams i mercifully
won't remember
so i never have to wake up
expecting to have you there.

Erotographomania: Love Letters to M.

Printed in Great Britain
by Amazon.co.uk, Ltd.,
Marston Gate.